HEAR TRAINS

CAROLINE KNOX

HEAR TRAINS

WAVE BOOKS

SEATTLE/NEW YORK

Published by Wave Books

www.wavepoetry.com

Copyright © 2019 by Caroline Knox

Wave Books titles are distributed to the trade by

Consortium Book Sales and Distribution

Phone: 800-283-3572 / SAN 631-760x

Library of Congress Cataloging-in-Publication Data

Names: Knox, Caroline, author.

Title: Hear trains / Caroline Knox.

Description: First edition. | Seattle : Wave Books, [2019]

Identifiers: LCCN 2018032876 | ISBN 9781940696805 (trade hardcover)

Classification: LCC PS3561.N686 A6 2019 | DDC 811/.54—dc23

LC record available at https://lccn.loc.gov/2018032876

Designed and composed by Quemadura

Printed in the United States of America

9 8 7 6 5 4 3 2 1

First Edition

Wave Books 075

HEAR
TRAINS

POMANDER

First of all, hold in your hand
a ripe *Citrus sinensis*,
sweet orange (of the rue
family), a fruit Chinese
in origin, and now
tropical. Circle this
globe with a ribbon,
make a bow and loop:
in Andrew Marvell's words,
"He hangs in shades the orange bright, /
Like golden lamps in a green night."

The clove: *caryophyllus*
is its name, a tongue twister,
like the clove itself, which is
the blossom's bud, culled and dried.
In Edward Taylor's words:
"The Clove, when in its White-green'd blossoms shoots, /
Some Call the pleasantst sent the World doth show."

To make a pomander,
grasp the orange gently, and

stud it entirely with lines of cloves
so no rind shows. Leave it to age and dry
days and months, a smaller emblem
of itself; a paradox of
acid and balm combined, so the fragrance
—sweet-tempered, good-natured—
pervades the air, the rooms, cupboards, and linen:
long-lasting, fresh, citric, and yet delicate.

until the springs had frozen totally over,
say February when the last birds and bugs
had fledged and flown. When the joe-pye weed
seven feet tall from all its deep nutrition in the springs
had turned gray and powdery and gaunt. Until the meadowsweet,
which is a wildcat spirea, had given up. I wouldn't mow it until
the ice could bear the machine, until it wouldn't buckle under,
and the baleful loosestrife had gone to seed.
Two tiny native orchids, *Spiranthes lacera gracilis* and *Habenaria lacera*
(slender, and torn), grow in the shade
of all these tough and taller species. Minute
colonies of mosses surround these orchids,
you wouldn't know they were there
if you didn't know they were there.

The neighbor who yearly mows this field was once a member of
some elite and corporate power structure; now he deliberately
guides an internal combustion engine forward and back across
field after field after field, a happy man, spring-ridden.

So *sault* means "jump," as in
sauter in France, but not
in New France! In Old France
the *l* dropped out. In New,
they kept it: Sault Ste. Marie,
the leap, the rapids. But
in a linguistic roux, *Sault*
became *Soo*, reduced. Very
practical, actually, like
semaphores or an aquifer.

Why, clouds needing airfoils
ballooned up over the skiff
portage under the overpass
of the Soo Line and north to the
Soo-Dominion connector,
as sailors to the top.
They say *skip* because the ship rolls;
hear trains while asleep slipping into foul-weather gear,
hear trains while asleep.

BONE GHAZAL

There is a handsome wildflower/weed, *Eupatorium perfoliatum*, bone-
set, which I worked my fingers to the bone

trying to transplant, without success. It bears white umbels—
umbrellas, really—and its blossom is the color of bone.

Alan Alda, they say, told a Columbia Physicians and Surgeons
commencement that "the headbone is connected to the heartbone."

The brother of Napoleon, seated on the throne of Spain,
was painted by Francisco Goya: this was Joseph Bon-

aparte, they say. Glamour and privilege; in those circles
they dined on the delicate veal sauce and marrow-bone

flavor of osso buco. You wouldn't find this dish in the
town of Robinson's masterpiece *Housekeeping*, Fingerbone,

Idaho. Boneset was used in home remedies, teas to assuage
pain of ague, flu and colds, indigestion in the elderly, bone

fractures. (Boneset tea! Catlap!) Alan and Arlene Alda gave so much
to help the world of poetry, I think there isn't a mean bone

in the body of either one. Goya painted masterpieces
galore, despite a tumor on the legbone.

This ghazal celebrates distinguished figures
whom I wish I had the musical talent to praise with the trombone.

on the campus of the University
of California at San Diego
among endearing neighbors:
Geisel Library, named for Dr.
Seuss, and cheek by jowl
with John Muir College,
named for the
pioneer naturalist and
ur-ecologist. Niki de
Saint Phalle *fecit*
1983. Curiously,
Sun God manages
to look both matte
and shiny at the
same time. It is a toy.
A man. A bird.
A woman, a bat.
It evokes Calder in its
"plain speaking." It
evokes poster paint.
Made of fiberglass,
its innards

mask a steel frame
in the public sculpture
garden, because *what*
is more public than light.
O, *Sun God*, shine
on us, we are
covered in gold leaf.

COLD BLOB

Make way, please, for the
cold blob; not "blog," it's
blob. Who is responsible
for this phenomenon: "The cold
blob may be a wild card";
"It is a large anomalous area";
"It is foreboding" [*sic*]; who is
the culprit? First identified,
if that's the right word, as low
salinity in rising oceans, the
cold blob is a colder surface
depth in the Atlantic called
AMOC! This stands for
Atlantic Meridional
Overturning Circulation.
"Amok" is much more like it.
Do you know what tongue
"amok" is from? It's Malay,
on the other side of the
globe. A disarranged self
runs amok, and is a wild
card, like the cold blob!

I may have read (some of)
this in the *Globe* (also called
the *Glob*). In mild ode mode,
a poem proceeds toward
a theme: causation, with
Physics and Chemistry
for Poets. A headline—
"The Water in Your Glass
Might Be Older Than the Sun."
The theory is, a cloud of ice
molecules predated and
then survived the sun.
Transparent, or semi-
transparent: water, glass,
and also stone, as here.
An ignorant woman said
to a geologist, What a
lovely fossil! He said, Oh,
it's a dendrite. She said, No,
a fossil, see the leafy
branches. He: Long ago,
the dendrite formed when
dirty water seeped
into the cooling, clear
liquid quartz. She: A fossil.
The kindly geologist said
nothing to this mind run

amok. I heard their words.
And, as xenon glows
from an electric field,
clarity is accountability:
the cold blob is a bold
gob, the result of global
warming on this erose
biome we call home.

that you can't write a whole poem in
comma splice, who would be in a position to
know, the tree trunk is covered with colonies
of creepy moss, the raisin bread is what you
don't like, she says Kenya but he says Keenya,
My father's a parson in Norfolk, Elizabeth
observed serious vertical rain, he's a jerk,
they wear the Laura Ashley laundry bags,
they *all* wear them, *Ralph Roister Doister*,
a tisane may be made in winter from rosemary
sprays or fennel seed, Muriel Rukeyser wrote
"No one ever walking this our only earth, various,
very clouded, in our forests, in all
the valleys of our earthly dreams," this may
be a list poem, it's nobody's business
if you want to write like this, a cousin was attacked
in the forest, if I were you I'd go through the
turnstile, *Jules porte le nouveau plateau*, let the
jussive subjunctive be used, she would be happy
with chocolate milk, polished paving stones were
once millstones grinding, no one has met Jugurtha,
our blood is being cleaned for us as we speak,

Ann will take a course in the Norwegian craft of
rosemaling, Velcro is the opposite of Teflon,
Melville knew New Bedford well, straits are a
dicey place for boats to shelter secretly,
children sang "There is a camel in my bed"
to the tune of "There Is a Tavern in the Town,"
Reggie read a biography of Stanley Baldwin,
define the "oblast," redingotes are obsolete,
she's earthy and sophisticated, we know that
the King Arthur legends reached Italy because
of the reliefs on the Modena Architrave, some
mammals are sponges, you think it's funny to
play mailbox baseball, 3.141592653589793,
antidisestablishmentarianism, forsythia is like a
school bus, the passive voice is looked down on,
the billiard balls when they carom off a side
with a bright dry crack shoot in another direction,

Sophia (a real person, not
an allegory) sat on the
top row of seats in
the amphitheater at
Ephesus. I stood
way down at the
center of the theater, below.
Sophia said Hello Caroline
quietly. I said Hello
Sophia quietly, this was
1959. We heard
one another exactly.
How great when a poem
does an extra job,
like Robert Morgan's
piece on *Poetry Daily*,
"History." He made *each*
and *teeth* rhyme. "History"
could go between any poem
and any other poem in a
book, on a screen, and would
ennoble the context. ("Ennoble

the context" is a code switch.)
Sophia and I, teenagers,
thought the context
of Ephesus was pretty
ennobled already, what
with Saint Paul and all
in Acts, and Artemis.
Morgan biographed
Daniel Boone, prolific
frontier hero in the
theater of the Seven
Years' War and else-
where, same age almost
as Washington, who was
there, too—how about
that? Whom Ron Chernow
biographed nobly.
Boone is the subject
of tons of fakelore
(Morgan set
the record straight),
and fakelore itself
is a form of code switch;
it's like decay, the half-life of radium.

See here, everybody,
have a good swig of
squid ink from a cobalt
ceramic mug. Have a
Windex martini! Such
behaviors foster visions:
Oh, blue, pastoral hue:
a welkin-eyed cow eats
niche-blue silage corn;
the blue part of blue cheese, it's
penicillin; Neruda blue, the
"cracking of the blue cold";
the Mel Gibson *Braveheart*
blue, he was woad wroth!
Mel made a first-rate
Hamlet, though, melancholy
blue. A bird could make
a blue egg for you, if a robin.
Is the turquoise named
for Turkey? Yes! Is
Turkey blue? What about
the Turkish navy? A man

dropped a navy blue
reference book on his
foot, which then turned
navy blue for a month
or two: what a booby.
Then in a blizzard
he put two blue *New*
York Times bags on his
feet before he put same
feet in waders. Amy
Clampitt saw in "Beach
Glass" the blue of both
Chartres and also Phillips'
Milk of Magnesia.
My sister and I, much
struck by the show at
the Worcester Art Museum
called *Cyanotypes*, which are
blueprints, thought we'd
make one, in an epic
project; we tried but failed
to follow the directions.
You should buy the
catalogue, *Cyanotypes*,
it's only $19.95.
The *New York Times* of
lines 29 and 30 above

addressed the Worcester
event: Ted Loos quotes
an expert, Dusan Stulik:
the blueprints "handle
subtle light well, and
they are fairly sturdy," on
02/05/16, C1. Further,
Kristina Wilson's catalogue
essay goes, "Our minds
play with the cyanotype's
iconicity, indexicality,
symbolism, and the deep,
affective power of its blue
tone." I had to google
"indexicality." This
found me in philosophy, and
happy to see blue as richly
useful, applicable in time
and space. But definitely must
now close this blue poem as shades
of cadmium, carbon, and slate
streak their DNA across
the night sky to sleep
deep as the blue Danube
down to the ocean azure
lapis lazuli, aqua, teal.

asked Mrs. Bladethorpe. "Oh," he replied, opening the door for her, "Frango mints; quinoa; Listerine; *Plain or Ringlets* by Surtees; a darning egg; black cumin; a plumb bob; thirteen conch shells in a sea-grass basket; a framed watercolor of unknown flowers; *Around America, a Cookbook for Young People* by Mildred O. Knopf; a kazoo; Craisins; bicycle clips for palazzo pants (Who is going to ride a bike in those?); a galvanized funnel; turquoise donkey beads; St. Francis surrounded by birds and crumbs, casein on pine board; calamine; spats; neat's-foot oil; and board games with many missing pieces."

His ancestor was a wandering Aramaean; his
forebear was a fugitive Sherpa; his anteced-
ent was a refugee biped; his forerunner was
a migrant upright mammal; his great-greatest-
uncle was a pioneer nomad; his footloose pro-
totype was an intrepid mountaineer; his peri-
patetic relative was a transcendentalist; his
muscle-bound cousin was a vagabond natu-
ralist; his genetic hero was a waterborne Le-
ander; his icebreaking kinsman was a spear-
throwing Aleut; his flaxen-haired grandam
threw a mean horseshoe; his aunt was a Spi-
noza-quoting equestrian sorceress; his venture-
some uncles were dribbling globe-trotters; his
wayfaring skylab was a peregrine falcon: so
"close and ancient," wrote John L. McKenzie,
SJ, were ties between Israel and Aram, and
"Space is disappearing and your singularity,"
    wrote Frank O'Hara, both of them right.

SONNET

Don't write in your books, said our parents,
except your name. So I did.
I wrote in them what the teacher said.
We read a poem full of small objects,
ordinary ones. James Hazard was
the teacher; he asked three students
to each read the poem out loud. He said, These objects don't
symbolize anything, they won't
lead to anything; they must be
there for their own sake. I wrote what he said
in the book margin. It turned out true ever after.
Example—Susan Firer, his wife, wrote in a poem:
The interruption of trees, of words, of nuns in Reeboks.

MANGANESE

After we had heard the notables
reading their poems at the Zinc Bar,
we went along to the Palladium Theatre,
presenting our gold and platinum cards for tix,
to wait for the curtain of *Arsenic and Old Lace*.
We both spoke Manganese so as not to be
understood. Some people have a tin ear,
as phosphorus glows in jellyfish at night.

Then we found out that our (chromium-adorned) (unlocked)
rental Mercury was stolen! When you need one,
where's the copper with a silver bullet
who could help you out on this one?
Or a Silicon Valley type with a whiff of sulfur,
as if the devil had been at hand. If I had a nickel
for every similar blunder I've made,
I could afford to send up a neon sign
on a helium balloon saying that
it was my ineptitude that led to all this.

SITTING

Have you met them? The unfinished
thoughts left visible—*non finito*—
in this show at the Met Breuer, visibly so:
works not finished by mistake,
and works not finished on purpose!
Is this what they want? Yes.
Go, the show is up until September 4.

Take your pick, but you can't have both.
Finishing is *sur le tapis*: Edna
O'Brien said, "The real self is
at the desk." The Met
poster depicts a Nam draftee
who sat for Alice Neel. Did not
come back for second sitting, did
not come back at all, mistake.

of the ramshackle ad hoc ranch house
pulled off all its siding and trim and improvements
and replaced them. Posh trucks came with imported
teak and mahogany, stained-glass panels appeared.
Balconies and terraces stretched out
everywhere. My brothers were yacking in the
front seat of the car, opining about the improved
improvements. Isn't it fortified now? Isn't it
imposing, protected, isolated? Isn't it embattled?
What do you make of the triforium? What's
a triforium? Corbels around oriels,
oriels around corbels. I was in the back-
seat doing email, pretending to work.
See the standing buttresses holding up the
flying buttresses. Look at the colonnade of caryatids
holding up the garage. What a residence.
Landscape overdesign has practically smothered it.
We drove back and forth looking (my brother
the driver addressing the packed traffic
as our mother did: Stop that, buster).
Isn't this domicile castellated?
Look at the mansard roofs on the

crenellated dormers. Oh, triforium
just means the gallery above the
windows. This house has become a duchy.
I can't remember which brother had once aimed
to be an architectural historian, but he flung
the nomenclature of the field around
at an early age, so the rest of us picked it up and
flung it around, too, and back at him. It was fun,
you weren't responsible for actually knowing
what you were talking about, but the rattle
and repetition made you feel part of
something large and important. Back then we
also collected useless facts:
our phone was 1763,
the end of the French and Indian Wars.
My sister, who wasn't in the
car, and I, both klutzy, were
born into a family of
serious athletes. Our
father was national amateur
squash racquets champ and
also runner-up (in separate
years). Our brothers were
always at practice of various
sports. My sister said to
me, You and I are throw-
backs! Fine with us. She

always called our
brothers our *bothers*,
it was a joke, they
were and are entirely
okay. Now on the occasion
of the current poem, one
brother was driving the other and me
(but not my sister—separate
car, because she had to teach)
to a meeting in Boston. Car trips,
especially day trips, are fine
spaces to exchange thoughts.
We drove past Wellesley,
where in our youth our
parents took us to stage plays.
We saw *The Seagull*. The ex-beauty
sat in an armchair leaned on
by the hero. Enter the Seagull,
the beautiful ingenue. Oh, said
the hero, isn't she beautiful.
The ex-beauty: Very prettily
dressed, and interesting-
looking. This was searing to
me! I remembered every word,
and knew their language was
a key to stories, poems, plays.
It was a relativity moment.

Here's what I always envied
the bothers: at their all-boys
school, they got to have Tintin
and his dog and adventures and
funny friends in French for their
FRENCH-CLASS TEXTBOOKS.
I was in the backseat
starting this poem.
At that school they were
taught by Mr. Eaton. What did
they secretly call him? Moth.

KIMONO

Seasons and chores are each and both very musical.
You can put on a kimono to participate in the first
(long) and the second (shorter).
I try to use the metal can open-
er in preparing supper. People
put the obi on the kimono to complete
its design, which makes for dignity. All
seasons have their own music. You must
not spill on the kimono, which was brought,
like a sail, from Asia by Colonel Treadwell.

BACK AND FORTH

in homage to Schiffer and Hindemith's Hin und zurück

ROBERT: Good morning, dearest. What's that printed paper?

HELENE: Oh, it's just—an email . . .

ROBERT: But what is in this email?

HELENE: Oh, it's just—an email of a poem, "Reversible Story," by Lydia Davis.

ROBERT: Sweetheart, you lie. *(Shoots her dead.)*

Deus ex Machina emerges from a trapdoor.

DEM: I come to you from above. True to my calling, I reverse the sequence of events. Occluded power rises from my words. *(DeM raises his arms in a stately gesture.)*

DEM: Ham index course, Mexican had cure. Diana muse chex. Unix Aida scheme: sachem, adieu!—N. Exude in a chasm, chained ex-Maus. Xmas inched AE. Ach, Ma, mixed Sue. In this connection, I can't recommend highly enough "Reversible Story," by Lydia Davis, collected in her *Can't and Won't* (FSG, 2014, 61). *(DeM waves around a copy of* Can't and Won't, *back and forth, flip-flop, and sinks back into trapdoor.)*

ROBERT: Sweetheart, you don't lie. (*Bullet goes back into gun. Helene gets up.*)

HELENE: Oh, it's just—an email of a poem, "Reversible Story," by Lydia Davis.

ROBERT: But what is in this email?

HELENE: Oh, it's just—an email . . .

ROBERT: What's that printed paper? Good morning, dearest!

CURTAIN

TRANSEPT

Their sound is gone out, belts out a choir
visible and audible here in the transept
North   East   West   South: acronym, NEWS
gone out   andante   *into all lands*
turf and twig. (An *OED* or google game
[*trans*—across; *septum*—enclosure],
as this item: "The pediment of the southern
transept [of Kiddington] is pinnacled,
not inelegantly, with a flourished cross.")
and their words   I keep reminding myself
unto the ends of the world   swept
aisles and isles going and coming either way
coming and going, monument and document.

LOOK,

Look, the Internet doesn't have a watermark
because it isn't print; it has a hashmark
and other terms, which earmark
IT experience as a birthmark.
Surfing, we deliriously benchmark
one foot in front of the other as in Telemark
skiing, which you don't find in Chilmark,
a hamlet on the Vineyard, a landmark
not of King Mark, but of the Prince of Denmark.
Semantic panache is the Internet's hallmark,
"masterly summings up of damn all," wrote Margery Allingham
in *More Work for the Undertaker* (McFadden Books, 1949, 27).

My father said *sine die*
meaning "no set date"
—We will adjourn sine die—
and pronounced it "synee dye."
It wasn't trig, it wasn't
dying. A lawyer he
was and my mother
a master of landscape
architecture (it was called).
She said *Sansevieria*
rei vieri, pronounced
"sonsa-veery-a
ree-eye vie-ear-eye."
It's a restaurant plant.
My husband was a canon
lawyer who said *Sede*
vacante nihil innovetur;
this meant if an office
is vacant, nothing must
interfere with the next
incumbent's freedom. In
grade school I had to take

lots of Latin, so I memo-
rized *Gallia est omnis*
divisa (I said "dee-wee-zah")
in partes tres, quarum
unam incolunt Belgae...
Belgians? Shouldn't Belgians
be Belsh? By analogy with
Welsh? For both are
somewhat Celtic, aren't they?

"I wouldn't have minded,"
wrote Katha Pollitt in
1984 (the year, not
the book)—"I wouldn't
have minded a little earthy
vulgarity, a few words
like 'bus conductor' or 'galoshes'
or 'margarine' among the
laurel wreaths and laments."
I've been carrying this
Pollitt insight around in
my head ever since,
and now it's on the screen.
Galoshes appears as
"goloshes" in Joyce's "The
Dead" (the story) and it's
how Angelica Huston
says it to her Gabriel
Conroy in *The Dead*
(the movie), in a veil
of disgust and scorn!
That is enchanting: "Goloshes!
Guttapercha things!"

Panels of dark green
on the pale green dress
she is wearing
(in the movie).
The overshoes were
made of rubber.
Gabriel did not
know who he was.
In the poem of power,
all you get is the
nature part and the
holes in the plot.
It's the absolute
key to how to
write, so that's why
most of the plot's
left out of "Down by the
Salley Gardens." I double-
dare you to sing it in
the car by yourself
without tears. All you
get is the nature part
and the holes in the
plot, that's the key,
like with "The Wife of
Usher's Well"—what's
with the bonny lass anyway
at the end of that one?

POLIS

Come into a city celebrated for its ring roads that are public art,
and you are implicated in the centripetal force of the polis.
Please notice the word *petal* hiding in centripetal; petals
radiate from a composite. Come into a municipality
and think about what a fancy word that is for city. Please
notice the word *pol* hiding in polis; please notice the word *is*, ditto.
Please notice the berms along ring roads and the strong cones
protecting you from construction danger. Nothing can
protect you from vertigo on the constant interchanges,
the whiplash as you might career over by inertia
into canals below. Canals are polluted. Canals and fountains:
think of the coins we have been unable to resist
flicking into fountains on this continent and others!
Vermin and disease! Come into a city plaza donated by a well-wisher
who wishes to remain nameless, but whose intelligent architect
planted green areas and pavilions and performance spaces,
playgrounds and restrooms. Mimes stand about miming.
How peaceful and reassuring, furthermore, is the street-grid,
in its beauty and sometimes, frankly, its restful boringness.
And here, finally, in the emphatic position, are the high-rise buildings,
which abide our wonder. Come into the magisterial
and funky vortex of this poem about a city,
which mentions hardly a single human being except you and me.

POPPITS,

which were invented in
the fifties and still exist,
were and are plastic
pearl necklaces that
you could pop apart
bead by bead and
reassemble to the
length that suited you;
opera, choker, bracelet.
The manufacturer
was Richelieu.

Pop it, an imperative
sentence. Contemplate
these decades. The sixties
followed what Alice
Adams called "the strictured
Fifties." In around
1962,
a man came up
behind my mother
at a party (she was

wearing poppits, *le
dernier cri*) and bead by
bead unpopped my mother's
entire necklace in front of
everyone and all the beads
rattled across the floor.

MIRROR

The ponderous oak frame—too shiny,
too grimy—in the secondhand store:
he bought it for a song

and brought it home. The frame
framed a colored engraving,
The Parting of Medora and Conrad,

by Pakenham. Who was Pakenham?
The work referred to a Byron poem,
"The Corsair." Well! he went to the mall.

There was GLASS HEAVEN. They replaced
the engraving with mirror glass.
He couldn't stop looking at his reflection.

HELEN

She remains important: think of Leni
Riefenstahl; Helena, Montana; Mount
St. Helens, with all its residue. Think
of Ellen Glasgow; *Eleni* (marvelous non-
fiction by Nicholas Gage). Think of all
those Arthurian Elaines, easy to mix up.
What about Lainie Kazan—she's a Helen too.
Was this the face that launched a thousand
ships? Yes, all of them bearing her name.

NUTHATCH SONG

"Well dressed," I
breakfast on in-
sects, which break-
fast on tree bark.
The speaker is a
nuthatch, that's
me. We are the
only birds to go
headfirst down a
tree. (Roger Tory
Peterson pointed
this out in *A Field
Guide to the Birds*,
Cambridge, MA,
1947, 164.)
*Sitta caroli-
nensis* is my name
in books. They aren't
concerned with nut-
hatches dying out.

We don't lean against our tails
the way woodpeckers do.
Oh, no, we don't lean against our tails
the way woodpeckers do.

To find our food, we
cram acorns and
nuts into bark, we
whack them open to
eat. This works, we
hatch the nuts and
then we all feast.
You will have no-
ticed that this song is
full of objective (if
random) infor-
mation on the nuthatch
experience. It all
comes from the web-
site of the Cornell Lab
of Ornithology,
allaboutbirds.org,
for which humans
and nuthatches are
and should be grateful.

                    Nuthatches are also grateful for sunflower
                    seed, suet, and peanut butter.
                    Oh, yes, we're also grateful for sunflower
                    seed, suet, and peanut butter.

On the Santa Ana winds this elevated group
soars, and at night by the light of St. Elmo's fire
they drift as far as Santo Domingo and beyond. You should
see them gyrating to "The Saint Louis Blues"
and "The St. James Infirmary"! The opposite of St. Bernards.

On breaks, this one reads *Four Saints in Three Acts*, by Stein;
that one is reading *Saint Joan*, by Shaw. A third is
reading *Mont-Saint-Michel and Chartres*, by Henry Adams. They are all
reading about themselves in *The Lives of the Saints*
in Saint-Tropez or St. Moritz, watering-places *de luxe*.

The saints make frequent use of the antidepressant and antioxidant
     St.-John's-wort.
Settling in with cases of Saint-Émilion, one of them retells
the riddle of "As I was going to St. Ives." Another recites
"The Eve of St. Agnes." One is immersed in Rumer Godden's
lovely novel *A Candle for St. Jude*. They dine on coquilles St.-Jacques.

And they think this is lots of fun, but extreme hedonism and extravagance
and cultural overload catch up with every one of them. So they go on the
     historic
pilgrimage—mountain and valley, desert and plain and swamp—to Santiago
     de Compostela.

POEM

The aoudad, a North
African sheep, doesn't
eat the fruit of the
baobab tree, a South
African native.
Chaos and
inchoate sound
like words related
to each other,
but of course they
aren't. Totally
different roots.
American Heritage
says *inchoate* is
from Latin for "not
yet harnessed." It
says *chaos* is from
Latin (and Greek) for
"empty space." Well,
both words are lovely
noises to dramatize
confusion. So are

ukes of koa wood,
a fine-textured
Hawaiian tree.
In Maori, the
particle *noa* means
all these words or
phrases: *only*,
just, *nearly*, *quite*,
until, *at random*,
idly, *fruitlessly*,
in vain, and *as soon as*.
Noa sounds like
an adverb to me.
What is it with
O and A—alpha
and omega?
I logged on to
AOL to see.
Aonia is where
the Muses live,
in Helicon. In
Italy, Aosta was
Saint Anselm's home-
town. The lifting
organ, the aorta,
carries blood to and from the heart.

A RUBRIC

A rubric stands out on the page in hot color.
Seraphs ornament its components, engrossed in the work,
stronger than brick dust (a basis for stain).
Not seraphs, idiot!—serifs!
—in manuscripts and early printed
books. Plenty of seraphs in the
Gothic illuminations, though.
The red introduces the
instructions, which are black.
You're supposed to follow them.

Stronger than brick dust, a rubric is
red earth, suggesting clay,
an ochre called a "ruddle,"
cheerful matte scarlet
"thus marking in a distinctive manner
that to which attention is to be drawn"
(says the 11th *Britannica*).
Sanguine, a rubric makes bold to say:

Here may be sung a
Song.

TARRAGON

To make a tarragon ode, you might address the effects
this fine herb has on the expansive senses.
See bright dark leaves, matte surfaces on
blowing stems and shoots. A green incense rises
from crushed foliage. For many ailments,
tarragon tea. For salad, infuse it with a vinegar:
a shade of anise, licorice. To hear it,
put your ear close to the plants,
let the wind come and brush the shoots together.
To hear it, think of the perfect rhyme in Aragon,
in France, where the best cultivars flourish.
Oh, wildly versatile multitasker,
you have such an unassuming flower.
Tarragon, tarragon, *Artemisia dracunculus*,
what are you doing over there among the
Compositae, the daisies? Sweet and piquant,
scratchily tactile, filling people's mouths,
filling them with binomial nomenclature.

black-and-white, with distinguished black freckles on the muzzle, and

one puppy, barely ambulatory, brown and white, slithered through the
    open screen door

when no one was looking, and charged into the living room. This room
    was in St. Louis, Missouri,

birthplace of T. S. Eliot and Marianne Moore, and it was large and full of
    comfortable

furniture. There were nice-looking worn rugs on the floor, and the two
    elder dogs

ran around and around on the rugs, crumpling them. They barked not one
    bark,

but hurled themselves faster and faster in a circle around the room,

messing up the rugs completely and dissociating them from their rug pads.
    The dogs were

shedding all the while. Then they went over to the fireplace and upended
    the woodbox and the

kindling basket. They knocked down all the fire irons on the granite
    hearth with horrible noise.

The smallest was absorbing all the methods of the elder dogs, who
    seemed to

know this. They knocked over one of those fancy matchboxes with long
    matches

that people sometimes give you as visiting presents. Fortunately these didn't
  ignite.
Then all three dogs were exhausted, so they crawled under the coffee table
  and slept.

This happened at my aunt Deirdre and uncle Leonard's house in St. Louis,
and I know because I was there, too, and the thing I liked best about the
  performance
was that Aunt Deirdre and Uncle Leonard sat on the sofa and laughed and
  laughed the whole time,
and they didn't tell the dogs to stop or call them bad dog or smack them,
and pretty soon the dogs went outdoors again and ran off into the bushes
  and down to the garage.

A WIDE BORDER

A wide border, a decorative orphrey,
a flange of deep shadow tones, honey, and wheat—
in two lines. One close to us, one
at some distance and thus smaller.

The men forming each line lean
as if affectionately toward one another,
helping to steady a neighbor: as the
sun sets, moon rises on the bleak palette
(a frieze pose, it seems, with
a ceremonial cast),

while all around the feet of these
two lines of standing men, close
to us and far off, other men lie down
or try to sit, bandaged heads, arms
in slings, unable to stand, a ground
cover of the wounded and the dead.

He painted the Pasdeloup
Orchestra, Mrs. Gardner, and Mrs.
Wertheimer; he painted Ellen

Terry, the daughters of Edward
Darley Boit, himself, Venice,
the Stevensons, Olmsted, Duse,
and John D. Rockefeller.
The painting is *Gassed*;
the date is 1919;
the painter is John Singer Sargent.

"Animals, an owl, frog, open their eyes, and a mirror forms on the
ground." So says Mei-mei Berssenbrugge. It might be life
on the river, the mirror of sky over us.
I start with a list because a water-
shed poem is quantitative, it's like-
ly to have a Quote List and a River

List; for example, "A river
is always giving ITSELF a bath" (in the
words of Kenneth Koch). Or to name rivers, like
the Thames or the Lucinda River, a life
of Cheever's swimmer in chlorinated water.
All this may seem sensible to us,

like the serious waterway thus
denominated by Stevens: "The River
of Rivers in Connecticut," moving water
from Canada to Long Island Sound, the
route of commerce and pleasure, a life
of broad reaches and falls alike,

where "the slow sea slaps slow water," like
Charles Bernstein says, continuous
and continual as the life
it harbors. Let the Shetucket River
join the Thames. We could see the
deep image of Diane di Prima's "as water,

silk / the quiver of fish," from the surface of the water.
We should hear Rusty Morrison's words "like
water-spiders on a pond the
hours pass overhead stop" as anxiety in us;
likewise Cole Swensen: "with a river
on the other side, another life."

Reading *Walden* is taking a course in life-
writing. Stevens called his water-
way a curriculum. A river
poem is qualitative, too. Thinking like
a grown-up, Thoreau assures us
as he nears the end of *Walden*: "The

life in us is
like the water
in the river."

TEX TILES

It was a parallelogram, it had four nice right

angles to it when I strung it on the loom; it was a

cream and green wool (with some synthetic)

place mat or a doormat, this art adventure—it was warp

interacting with weft or was it woof? It started as

the fiber oblong, but haste and inexperience

with impatience verging on dislike

made me pull my medium in ugly yanks of hanks

in each direction to and fro until I found

Oh woe! my web was in the shape of

the Lone Star State and I was

in a state myself. What could I

make of my textile. Nothing.

So I took serious instruction from a potter

and fired a tile in low relief and incised writing

of the prehistoric pictographs at Hueco Tanks,

near El Paso; a tile of the Mound Builders at

Caddo Mounds, near Nacogdoches; a tile of

the first map of Texas, by Álvarez de Pineda

in 1519; and a tile of the coming of the Sieur de La Salle in 1684.

People with occupations, which is to say vocations,
callings, like a cinematographer who shares his expertise,
kindly providing directions to show the sewing-machine
repairman how to make an omelet: such people
light the way. The omelet is filled with asparagus
and soft cheese. The repairman gets good at this sharing,
and shows a children's librarian how to
strip wallpaper. The librarian is seeing an ichthyologist,
who tells his chimney sweep the plot of *For Whom the Bell Tolls*.
The chimney sweep makes a dollhouse croquet set for the
cinematographer's granddaughter; the man who grew the
asparagus for the omelet is a college classmate of a
School Sister of St. Francis who is happy to
tell a dry cleaner how to cross the Bear Mountain
Bridge without getting acrophobia. Bird camp
is where they met. A breeder of West Highland
terriers instructs a CPA on affordable
stamp collecting. All these light the way:
a piano tuner, who is also a notary public and a limo driver,
imparts the gnosis of artisanal beer
to a self-storage entrepreneur whose mother and father before him
had once each been both crane operators and flamenco dancers.

Glorious Apollo from on high beheld us, such as we were and are, *wand'ring to find a temple for his praise* (temple?!). *Sent Polyhymnia* (Who but she?) *hither to shield us* (Shield from what?). In any case, under the auspices of Polyhymnia, sing we a hymn by Sabine Baring-Gould: "Now the Day Is Over"; sing we a hymn by Julia Ward Howe: "I can read His righteous sentence in the dim and flaring lamps." —Okay, *Sent Polyhymnia*, and sing we in the Lake District "Hymn to Intellectual Beauty" by Shelley. Sing we everywhere "A Hymn to God the Father" by Donne anywhere. *Glee and good humour our hours employ*, except when they employ sarcasm, rancor, envy, and self-righteousness. *Thus then combining, hands and hearts joining—* Hold hands while singing? We have to hold sheet music! Do we put hand over heart? *Sing we in harmony*; sing we in Acapulco, sing we in Des Moines! Sing we in Burbank, waltzing Matilda; sing we in Harmony (in Maine and Minnesota), sing we in Harmony (in N.J. and R.I.), oh sing we in Delphi *Apollo's praise.*

CATARACT

Tear-streaked mascara, mascara-stained cheeks: a cataract of woe, of woes, pouring gravity. Oh, frozen heart making new meltwater. The intromitting cascades are downspouts to bedrock erosion by rain within the meaning of the act; oh, they're crestfallen runnels to disgusting scum and mist in an eddy. They're stop-and-go freshets as from some (extrusive aqua plastic) waterslide estuary. To proceed: through acqueous humor to the cataract! And excised foam, simultaneous blur and cloud. The eyes are three weeks apart. Minneapolis has introduced a spillway, dam, and locks at its natural waterfall, to promote commerce. And this commerce has led to an acrylic model of the cataract.

PHEASANT-EYE

A ring around your elegant, indignant eye,
a ring collar around your neck:
"Courting males utter a loud double
squawk followed by a whir of
wings (not audible at a distance)."
You are an interesting and beautiful
bird, pheasant, but you should know
that pheasant-eye is also the
name of a narcissus. Does that
make you less narcissistic,
birdbrained bird? You fly
in the brush and wind and high
air; the bulb lies in deep loam
and moves so slowly. You,
blessèd bird, fare north "only
as far as deep snows will allow,"
but said deep snows protect
and excite said bulbs to
flower. Unbeknownst, you
probably even pass these
namesakes as you whir
through underbrush and

overbrush. (*Overbrush*
is also a dentist word—
Don't overbrush, bad
for enamel.) But you
who are *Phasianus*
colchicus—this is your
Latin name—you are the
Phasian bird, from the
River Phasis in ancient
Colchis, which may be Turkey
today. (Pheasant comes
from Turkey?) Now please
let us segue to Audubon.
Bird obsession is like no
other addiction: as when a
field full of otherwise sensible
grown-ups inanely waves and
bellows goodbye goodbye
goodbye to flocks of geese,
who reply GAWK GAWK
GAWK GAWK. Audubon
mentions pheasant in his
journals, but I can't find that
he painted you. Why not?
with your color, texture, and
carriage. So Audubon should
have gone to Alexander

Pope's pastoral "Windsor
Forest," and read aloud
thoroughly several times
lines 111–118, to
see and hear pheasant
life, a most moving passage,
such as inspires painting,
which is meant to tell us
who we are. After all,
Audubon painted the ruffed
grouse, didn't he? Pope
doesn't flinch—he tells us the
prey's despair: the pheasant
"feels the fiery wound /
Flutters in blood, and
panting beats the ground."
Who thinks of Pope as
an environmentalist?
There are high-toned works
such as *Too Late the Phalarope*
by Alan Paton or *A Phoenix
Too Frequent* (Christopher
Fry), evoking famous birds,
but most books about pheasants
are how to kill them. Your
elegant, indignant eye,
pheasant, is a target.

So I went off and read
"The Birds of America,"
by Rod Smith, collected
in *Touché* (Wave, 2015, 3),
which references a "tall
beach" and "honed
windows & grates."
I was comfortable
with that, admiring.

doorless and dark banker's gray with mold and/or mildew all over it;

it leaned against the air. Our host said, after we had eaten too much

Thanksgiving dinner, that he had been thinking of a bonfire

for this shed, and perhaps tonight was the time?

Since there had been rain recently, it would be safe.

There were the host's and hostess's families, cousins, grown-ups and
  children,

and a lot of people who they were I have no idea, plus dogs.

The shed had been in the newspaper because decrepit.

Couldn't some of it be saved? Our host ignited the fire with old engine oil,

and then the flames took off and up—they climbed

a ziggurat, seeming to enjoy it, a ziggurat

supported by a colonnade, bases and capitals; then pylons

reaching to flaming minarets, to campaniles. All frangible,

fungible, all close to being air already, ready, leaning on air.

Embers glow because the matter is hot enough to emit incandescent light.

I bet there were thirty of us sitting in beach chairs and lying on tarps and
  blankets,

and we didn't talk at all, we didn't laugh, and we certainly didn't sing.

We gazed into the practical and changeable flames and embers, and these
  reflected back on us.

ACKNOWLEDGMENTS

"Transept," "Latin Poetry"—*Divine Magnet*

"Look," "Back and Forth," "*Sun God* appears,"
"Glorious Apollo"—*New American Writing*

"Tex Tiles," "I wouldn't mow the field"—*Soundings East*

"Hear Trains," "Cataract"—*Narrative*

"Pheasant-Eye," "Who is going to tell you," "The new owners,"
"Helen," "Nuthatch Song"—*Forklift, Ohio*

"Double-Dare," "A wide border"—*Map Literary*

"Polis," "Poppits,"—*Tin House*

"Tarragon"—*Anchor*

"Two middle-aged springer spaniels," "Poem,"
"Saints Partying," "Bone Ghazal"—*Superstition Review*

"People with Occupations"—*Sixth Finch*

"Blue Poem" (in somewhat different form), "Pomander"—*Yew Journal*

"Code Switch," "A Rubric"—thecommononline.org

"Watershed," "Manganese," "Who"—*Hanging Loose*